REACH & EXCEED YOUR SALES GOALS

Using PRO$PERITY Personality Recognition

RON STICKLER

Reach & Exceed Your Sales Goals, Using Prosperity Personality Recognition
©2018 by Ron Stickler

Published in the United States of America by:
Prosperity Personality Recognition Publishing
5239 Country Squire Way
Fort Collins, Colorado 80528

Editor and Alchemist: Robin Shukle
Design and Production: Liz Mrofka
Cover Graph: Max Borovkov
Printed by: CreateSpace

LEGAL DISCLAIMER: No part of this book may be reproduced or transmitted in any form or by any means, electronic or mechanical, including photocopying, recording or by any information storage and retrieval system, without written permission from the author. You may not reprint, resell or distribute the contents of this book without express written permission from the author.

All violations will be remedied with legal action and justice will be sought to the maximum penalty allowable by law in the State in which the original purchaser resides.

ISBN-13: 978-1719408608
ISBN-10: 1719408602

REACH & EXCEED YOUR SALES GOALS

Using PRO$PERITY Personality Recognition

RON STICKLER

PROSPERITY
PERSONALITY RECOGNITION
PUBLISHING

Table of Contents

Preface 6
Introduction 8
Client Testimonials 8

■ PART ONE
Basic Training 11

1 The Foundation of Personality Recognition 13
2 How Are People Wired? 15
3 The Manure Story 17
4 Sell Like a Chameleon 19
5 Rifle vs Shotgun Approach 21
6 What Types Are You? 23

■ PART TWO
Personality Traits 25

7 The Driver Personality 27
8 The Analytical Personality 31
9 The Craftsman Personality 35
10 The Persuader Personality 39
11 More Trait Recogntion 43
12 Levels of Personality Traits 47

13 Wants and Needs 51
14 DOs and DONT's 55
15 Personality Percentages 59

■■ PART THREE
Extra Valuable Tidbits 61

16 Match The Personality to the Job 63
17 Advertising to the Different Personality Types 65
18 Choosing a Seat at the Table 69
19 Bosses 71
20 Two Ears and One Mouth 73
21 Sell—Don't Tell 77
22 The Art of Mirroring 81
23 Have a Good One 85

■■ PART FOUR
Saving the Best for Last 87

24 Planning Your Sales Attack 89
25 Dominant Buying Motives 95

A Special Gift 99
Dedication 101
Acknowledgements 102
Now, Go Forth and Reach & Exceed Your Sales Goals 103

Preface

This book is written for sales people who want to improve their sales success and for sales managers who want to motivate their sales staff to achieve company goals. Once readers master the secrets of personality recognition outlined in this book, the rewards of prosperity, accomplishment, admiration and recognition will be theirs. Understanding the needs and wants of various personality types will result in a more effective dialogue, a higher closing percentage and, most importantly, a clearer understanding and a common purpose—the keys to a trusting relationship marked by success. Interested? Read on.

I have been in the sales field for more than forty years of my professional career. After college, I started out in the retail sales field with the J. C. Penney Co. I began as a trainee, was promoted to an Assistant Department Manager, and later became a full Department Manager.

But I felt the position did not offer the kind of exciting career I had envisioned. Bored and unchallenged, I gave notice and moved on. When I left Penneys, I adopted the motto that has guided my life ever since: "If you're not having fun, don't do it!" I have always believed—if you are a great salesperson, a job will open up because the supply is low, and the demand will always be high.

After eleven years as a wholesale representative with Zenith, I moved to a new job in 1984. I became a representative for Fairfield Communities. I had great self-confidence and a solid work history to support my credentials. I felt this position would offer me the breakthrough I had always wanted.

My timing was perfect! They were hiring for the busy summer season, and I had been on a full commission income in the past and loved it. The company sent about a dozen of us, all rookies, on an all-expense paid stint to their training facility. They invested a lot of money in preparing all of the new hires for a lucrative future.

I returned to work all pumped up, ready to start selling and making a lot of money. Soon reality taught me the company had invested all of their money in teaching me about *the product* itself, but nothing about the nitty-gritty of *HOW TO SELL* the product! Within a few weeks, my lack of sales put me close to being fired. I watched other new salespeople being let go, and feared for my job as the turnover increased.

I figured it would be *only a matter of time* before I would be summoned to the Sales Manager's office and dismissed. Luckily, fortune intervened. The company hired a consultant to present a special two-day seminar to the entire sales staff. The seminar focused on how you: 1) recognized and 2) sold to the different personality types.

I had never even heard of this strategy before, but after the seminar, my entire approach to sales changed. After the training, I put the information to use and became one of their top salespeople for most of the next decade. After leaving that job, I became one of the top real estate agents in my hometown for the next few years.

The *power* of understanding and using this information turned me into an immensely successful sales person. I used it for the rest of my career, winning multiple sales awards, living in personal luxury, and attaining every dream and goal I could imagine.

I enjoy sales because I love helping people. I also love teaching. Before getting my degree in business, I considered entering the educational field. These insights can be life-changing and significant, and I believe these insights are as basic as learning math and English in school.

The information embedded in the pages of this book is indispensable to both the salesperson and management. If *knowledge is power*, then understanding and using this approach will reveal the secret of success and provide the power to give an individual the self-confidence and ability to achieve every imaginable dream and individual goal.

Introduction

Something that makes personality recognition—even more—a part of your life—forever—and help you learn to relate certain traits and actions, likes and dislikes to a particular style (or types) = USE YOURSELF as a great 'barometer/gauge'.

Once you realize which mixture of personality types **YOU** are (and be very honest with yourself), you can enjoy recognizing similar traits in others which relate to your own style, and you will then understand much more about their motives.

Because if you realize something *you* like or don't like/do or don't do —guess what! Other people of that same style probably behave and think in the same way. That recognition ability helps you tremendously!

Another fun fact: by definition, people that are 'best friends' share some common traits in their personalities—and like-wise, often in physical appearance. Not necessarily exact, but very similar.

I'll never forget when I was walking through a mall and there were 3 young teenage girls walking together. All 3 were 1) very talkative 2) had long straight—similar colored (natural)—hair and 3) were quite similar in their physical appearance = no surprise to me !

FACT: People are 'more comfortable'/enjoy being around people they feel are a lot like themselves—in some ways—or in a lot of ways.

That is the basis of selling and personal behavior using personality recognition.

Client Testimonials

Ron's grasp of personality recognition is 'expert' in my opinion. He has taught my agents to recognize the different personalities of their clients, resulting in better relationships and more sales.
—Jim Smith, Managing Broker, Jim Smith Realty

Ron's lessons are incredibly valuable. I highly recommend him to anyone seeking to improve their management and leadership skills!
—Eric Thompson, President
Windermere Real Estate Services Colorado

Ron's personality information material has given our sales team the competitive advantage needed to become an elite selling force.
—Luke Barnes, Chief Sales Officer, Madwire® & Marketing 360®

I made a $2,300 sale the NEXT DAY after using what I learned with the Prosperity Personality Recognition information. My closing ratio has increased from 50% to 80%.
—Tim Washburn, Owner, Computer Doctors

After learning Prosperity Personality Recognition, our company's closing percent went up over 50% and our sales cycle was cut in half.
—Allan Ronquillo, Realtor
(past owner & CEO of Housing Helpers Real Estate)

Ron's concepts will change your sales career immediately! I closed my next 13 sales in a row after being introduced to Prosperity Personality Recognition.

—*Mark Weeden, Owner, Weeden Insurance*

I am seventy-one years old and have been in the sales field for forty-six years. I feel this information was the best sales information I've ever had.

—*Harley Patterson, Sales Rep. Schroll Custom Cabinets*

Ron's information DOUBLED my sales success due to how I now view my client. In my business, you usually only get one chance to make the sale, and this information made a huge difference and helped tremendously!

—*Wes Killion, Automotive Sales*

If you are looking to increase your closing ratio, or become a better leader, I highly recommend you purchase this book. This should be a required read for anyone in sales."

—*Deanne Mulvihill, Executive Director, Berthoud Chamber of Commerce, District Manager, Arbonne Intl.*

Ron's book has many points that can improve your sales and create an impactful mission to your business. I would rate this book as one of the top self-improvement books to read and a 'must have'!

—*Shawn Kastle, Insurance Agent & Owner of Kastle Insurance.*

PART ONE

Basic Training

1

The Foundation of Personality Recognition

Several famous individuals have worked with the analysis of personality types, including Freud, Jung and Maslow. These studies occurred within the past one hundred years, creating an increasing interest in the subject, but the study of personality types goes back much further.

Aristotle, Plato and Hippocrates studied personality types in the fourth and fifth century *BC*. Anything written more than 2400 years ago and still used by many people on a daily basis must be worthwhile.

Most personality studies divided various specific types into four groups. Although researchers give types different names, the similarity of characteristics and traits within each group show great consistency. The titles assigned to the different types were assigned in an attempt to help individuals relate to their specific type. Some types correspond with colors, animals, nature or fluids, but a close analysis of each set reveals similar analysis or description. The personality titles given to the four types in this book are the Driver, Persuader, Craftsman, and Analytical.

Each person displays various degrees of intensity of the different types. A person rarely exhibits only a single style, but is usually a mixture of two or more types. A trained observer can usually identify the individual's dominant characteristic within seconds of watching or talking with him/her.

Personality recognition can be extremely accurate in revealing the strengths and weaknesses of an individual's thinking, communicating and information processing traits. An astute manager who recognizes personality style traits can use that information by hiring the best person for a particular job, as well as enhancing the ability to get the most work quality from that person. With a good degree of certainty, management can also predict how an individual employee will perform a particular task or assignment.

Knowledge of personality traits can be used by every salesperson to better sell themselves, their ideas and their products or services. The benefits of such insights are endless. With personality recognition, an individual cannot actually read minds, but may accurately predict what a person will say or do.

Once personality dominance has been identified, the salesperson will know how individuals think, act or perform daily activities. Most importantly, the salesperson will know why the client will or won't purchase a product or service, and can modify their presentation to respond to those motives.

2

How Are People Wired?

Some people are motivated, or wired, completely differently than others. As a manager, salesperson or promoter, one must realize some employees will be motivated by money, awards or prizes, while others may be encouraged by job benefits, such as insurance or savings plans.

Have you ever driven or walked by a store and thought: *How do they stay in business? I would never even go in there because I have absolutely NO interest in what they are selling.*

Yet, these stores sell enough products to keep operating. If these stores have been open for a long time, evidently other people go there and buy what they are selling because those people have different needs and wants. We all make different choices, have unique tastes and like specific stores based on some inner feeling of satisfaction that comes when shopping there. These differences drive the economy and create buying trends that marketing companies spend millions of dollars trying to read. Those differences include: unique choices in cars, clothes, food, various merchandise, houses, etc.

Knowledge of the four personality types will help the salesperson pinpoint the needs and wants of buyers without spending millions of dollars on market research. In the future, advertisements, sales presentations and company training sessions can focus on the needs of individual clients based on the insights of personality types and not on 'hunches.'

In the following chapter, the salesperson will learn how differently people may view the very same thing. The brain is truly an amazing instrument!

3

The Manure Story

This is a short story about four people who enter a room separately and find a pile of manure on the floor. Using the labels for each personality style expanded upon in future chapters, you will get a preliminary glimpse of each type by the way the various individuals react.

A person with a Driver personality enters the room first and says, "This stinks! What the _____ is this doing in here? Someone tell my secretary to get it cleaned up immediately!" (Small details are often handled by a Driver's hired assistants.)

The second person to enter the room has an Analytical personality and says, "No one touch this. It could be dangerous. We need to analyze it thoroughly and determine if it is safe. If it is, we'll proceed." (Thorough analysis ensures certainty. The time needed to examine the findings is of little importance.)

An individual with a Craftsman personality arrives next and comments, "This discovery may be really good. I recommend the team gets together and suggests the benefits of this encounter." After the team input is gathered over a lunch meeting, the group decides to transfer the manure to a wheelbarrow and put it in the company garden area to help the flowers grow even better.

Finally, a person with a Persuader personality enters the room while the team is collaborating at lunch, sees the manure and cheerfully announces, "There must be a PONY around here somewhere. This is GREAT!"

Four different perspectives of the same issue. The story is a simple analogy to remind each reader that people see the product and service presented to them in unique ways and will choose to BUY or not and have various degrees of interest based on personality style.

Understanding the detailed information about personality types will explain how different types think about *everything*. Once familiar and comfortable with the details of each style, it will be much easier to identify the salesperson's 'target market,' permitting time and money to be invested more wisely with the right client.

Familiarity with personality style traits is not like mind reading, but comes fairly close. Knowledge of personality types, behaviors and language patterns will help the effective salesperson predict more accurately what a client likes and can adjust a sales presentation to meet perceived needs and wants. This information helps salespeople **KNOW WHY ANYONE BUYS ANYTHING, RESULTING IN A MUCH HIGHER CLOSING RATIO!**

4

Sell Like a Chameleon

People are much more likely to buy or accept whatever is being offered, if they perceive the sales person to be *like them*. Think about it. The last time you bought something, you most likely walked away saying to yourself: *I liked that salesperson. They were super. I'll try to send them some more business. That store is great!*

When you did not buy what the salesperson sold, you probably thought the opposite: *I had a bad feeling about them from the beginning,* or *they didn't understand what I wanted at all* or *that was a lousy salesperson.*

We buy things from people we like, and don't buy things from people we don't like. Who do we tend to like most often? Very simply, people who we feel are like ourselves. That impression often leads us to accept more of everything the other person says or does, which usually results in a sale.

What happens when we interact with people we don't like? Frequently the interaction ends due to a difference in thoughts, or perceptions of what is important and what is not. Sometimes the failure of a potential deal may be the result of words exchanged or perceptions of what the message is about. The 'deal breaker' may be the perception of a salesperson's demeanor, behavior, dress, or general appearance. All can make a huge difference in the success of the business encounter.

Salespeople want, no, actually need, as much working in their favor as possible to complete a deal. So, it is critically important to be aware of the small things that each personality style deems important. An insignificant mannerism or phrase may seem unimportant to you, but it may be essential to the client. *It's all psychological.*

This is why most successful salespeople have mastered the secret of using a personality style that matches the personality of their client. They become **chameleon-like**, using the ability to change *their* outward appearance and delivery to match their surroundings and client.

The change may only be required for a short time, depending on the degree and intensity of client interaction. An astute salesperson will make a shift in behavior and language to let the client know the needs and values of the client are understood. Actions that reflect an understanding of the client's needs and wants will markedly increase the success of the sale.

Only the Driver and Persuader can perform this transition without creating internal stress. The other two types, the Analytical and Craftsman, who do not like any type of change, require a more structured, predictable environment in which to function with minimal risks.

Once the Driver or Persuader learns how to recognize each personality style, they will also know what to say and do in a leadership role, and they will know what to do to convince others to follow their wishes. This eventually leads to the achievement of success, increased sales and a loyalty to the company, product or service being offered.

5

Rifle vs. Shotgun Approach

Salespeople often become creatures of habit. When they do something that ends with a positive result, they most likely say and do the same thing the next time a similar situation occurs, whether it's only a minute or a day or a week later.

If the positive result is a closed sale, the salesperson, without knowledge of personality recognition thinks: *When I said (or did) this before, it worked well, so it will probably work again.* If the results were not positive, they may say to themselves, *"Oh well, you can't win them all. I'll just keep trying."*

This is an example of **'the shotgun approach.'** When a shotgun is fired at a target, a scatter pattern of pellets occurs. Some may hit the exact center of the target, and some miss by a little or a lot. Salespeople will use the shotgun approach and 'win some and lose some' with little or no consistency.

On the other hand, **'the rifle approach'** yields more positive results. Instead of giving the client a sales presentation that works some of the time, the salesperson's knowledge of personality types finds the bullseye much of the time. The target has been designed by the seller to resonate with words, visuals and actions so the client accepts and responds to it with a 'yes' attitude.

Using personality style clues, 'the sale' combines the salesperson's personality, an idea, a product, or a service and matches them with the wants and needs of the client. These insights will lead to more profit, less stress and greater success.

The analogy of the hammer and the hardware store also supports this point. No one in history has ever taken a hammer back to a hardware store complaining, "It doesn't work." If the objective is to pound a nail into a piece of wood, it's going to work, that is, if you know how to hold it and how to use it. Familiarity with personality recognition is similar. Knowing the secrets of the system and how to use them is extremely effective. Successful closings will improve, often dramatically.

6

Which Type Are You?

There are four basic personality types. To better understand their similarities and opposite characteristics, it helps to think of the alignment of the various personalities as shown below. The image could be rotated, but just think of the types like this:

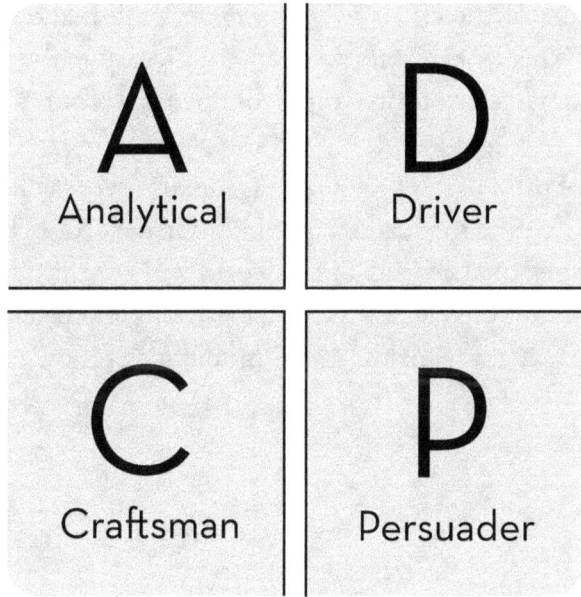

Important note: Similarities in personality style frequently occur in adjacent quadrants. For example, the Analytical and Craftsman types (**A/C**) share some similar qualities and characteristics, as do the Analytical and Driver (**A/D**) etc.

The Driver and Persuader (**D/P**) or the Analytical and Craftsman (**A/C**) find it easier to communicate with each other because they often use the same language and understand each other.

However, the Driver and Craftsman (**D/C**) and the Analytical and Persuader (**A/P**) are **direct opposite** types—opposite in every way imaginable. When dealing with a personality style that is one's exact opposite, it is essential to know how to interact with such a person, adapting language, approach, and actions to meet *their* needs, not the salesperson's style.

To clarify the point even further, whatever the Driver likes, the Craftsman dislikes, and vice versa. And what an Analytical likes, the Persuader dislikes, etc.

People are usually a mixture of two types with one more dominant than the other. The essential task for a salesperson is to recognize the dominant traits of the client *at that moment* and make the necessary adjustments to present the sale accordingly. Occasionally, an individual exhibits characteristics of three types, but never all four.

In Part Two of this book, each of the personality types will be discussed in detail. By the time the reader completes the next four chapters, both business and personal aspects of the world will appear quite different. The reader will notice several personality patterns and behaviors through new insights. Get ready for the "Aha" moment to follow.

PART TWO

Personality Traits

7

The Driver Personality

Drivers have the ability to make quick decisions without fear, hesitation or emotion. Their primary focus is on themselves, fame and fortune. Goal achievement plays a major part of the Driver's motivation.

Every opportunity offers the Driver a chance to succeed, and action is much more important than details. The Driver employs others to handle all details.

A Driver can be described as a decision maker, egotistical, dominating, abrupt, a workaholic, outcome-oriented and someone who wants/demands control and power. They think only of themselves, enjoy insulting or needling people and always say exactly what they mean. Consequently, they lack people skills and have a basic disdain for others.

A dominant Driver may *pretend* to care about others, but frequently *uses others* to achieve their own personal goals. Some Drivers are as infamous as they are famous. In movies and fiction novels, Drivers are characterized as villains. Dictators are usually Drivers who *take* power rather than being elected into it.

They will use phrases like: 'Take it or leave it,' 'It's my way or the highway,' or 'Just give me the bottom line.' They measure everything by one thing: RESULTS. The Driver only needs to be 51% correct to feel content.

Their ability to handle stress and make quick decisions motivates Drivers to choose occupations that encourage and require this characteristic.

It can lower your stress tremendously, when interacting with a Driver, if you adopt the philosophy: 'Don't take everything personally' because it's probably not personal! They are just being a Driver.

Any single characteristic/description can apply to two types, but two characteristics can narrow the choice down to only one type.

For example, in cue words of a Driver = 'forceful/direct' can also apply to a Persuader. In that same list of cue words = 'thinks only of self' could also apply to an Analytical.

But, if you were describing a person who was a leader and 'feared' by almost everyone = that would *only* be a Driver.

Of course, all of the words and phrases, on that page, would apply to a Driver.

Another Example: A 'very 'detailed person' could describe an Analytical OR a Craftsman. But if you add to that description = "who is very talkative'—that would *only* be a Craftsman.

Note: The second type which would be applicable, must always be an adjacent type in the main image—NEVER an opposite type! Opposites would also be the Persuader and the Analytical.

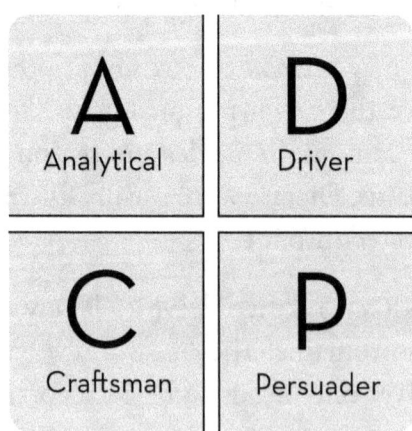

In other words, a Driver is similar to an Analytical in some ways and a Persuader in other ways, but 'totally opposite' of a Craftsman.

That's the way it is in life, as well. Whatever the Driver 'likes' or how they behave is totally opposite of a Craftsman, etc.

As time goes on, the more you understand personality recognition, the easier it will be for you to decipher which single description could also be describing another type.

CUE WORDS TO DESCRIBE THE DRIVER

Main decision maker	Thinks only of self
Egotistical	Workaholic
Hard, tough	Outcome oriented... *'bottom line'* thinker
Dominating, aggressive	Forceful, direct
Abrupt	Looks for challenges
Wants to control/have power	Cynical

BEHAVIORAL TENDENCIES

- Competitive in sports and work
- Wants more... the biggest, the best
- Gives orders rather than takes them
- Enjoys insulting or needling people
- Pleasant and generous as long as they are getting results
- Says exactly what they mean

FEARS

- Being taken advantage of
- Failure (is never an option!)

Some famous and infamous Drivers include: Steve Jobs, Elon Musk, Idi Amin, Adolf Hitler, Ho Chi Minh, and Saddam Hussein.

Important note: Please understand: the previously mentioned Drivers were 'extremely High Drivers.' Fortunately, there is a very small percentage of those people. A Driver, balanced with Analytical or Persuader personality traits (which is usually the case), can be an 'upstanding individual.'

VALUABLE TIDBIT: Be very careful—they equate talking a lot with insincerity and a waste of time. This hint is aimed at all of the Ps and Cs.

8

The Analytical Personality

Analyticals are detail oriented and analytically minded. These individuals are not socially oriented and tend to hide their emotions. Analyticals *infrequently* laugh, cry, hug, touch others, converse or show anger in public.

They make decisions based on facts and not emotions and always 'play by the rules.' Their high attention to details and meticulous efforts can make them exceptional employees.

The Analytical prefers working alone, having very little social contact with other employees. They can perform the same task day after day and love it. Analytical employees seek a job with good benefits and as much job security as possible. They show loyalty to the company, and they will often remain at the same job and organization for many years.

The Analytical will always be an **employee** rather than an **employer** unless they have at least half a personality mixed with Driver traits, which adds leadership. Analyticals don't want the stress of being an employer. Quick and multiple decision-making demands would add far too much stress to their lives.

The Analytical will always prefer to work on a salary rather than on a commission. Not risk takers, they prefer predictable patterns. Other employees see the Analytical as a solid, conservative person who, despite being somewhat rigid, could be counted on as a steady worker.

They are tradition-minded and resist any type of change in their lives. The Analytical's need to double and triple-check everything for accuracy can frustrate co-workers and managers. They fear being wrong at any task.

Typical Analytical positions include: accountants, inventors, research technicians, doctors and artists. They practice safety with every move.

They are conservative in every aspect of their lives.

CUE WORDS TO DESCRIBE THE ANALYTICAL

Accurate	Analytical
Systematic	Genius prone (thirst for detail)
Reserved/formal	Careful
Resists new ideas	Meticulous
Rigid	Conservative
Prone to be suspicious	Perfectionist

BEHAVIORAL TENDENCIES

- Make lists and checks items off as completed
- Traditional (conscientious . . . strong feelings about right and wrong)
- Likes preset standards and systems
- Resistant to change
- Extremely loyal
- Avoids exposure to changes, new things and danger
- Itemizes everything. Has multiple checklists
- Cautious about taking chances
- Must double-check everything for accuracy

FEARS

- Criticism

- Being wrong

Well-known 'High Analytical' characters: Mr. Spock of *Star Trek* fame, or Adrian Monk from the former TV show, *Monk*.

Others view them as *quiet nerds* who operate *'below the radar.'*

In the grand scheme of things, they play an important role where details matter. The Analytical prefers to play this part and keep 'doing the right thing' to make their view of the world work.

9

The Craftsman Personality

The Craftsman is a patient person who enjoys routine in life. They are followers rather than leaders and *'go by the book'*—following *the rules of life*, and every specific job procedure in the employee work manual.

As a result, the Craftsman often chooses a job that requires many of these traits. A Craftsman can make an excellent secretary or assistant because of their attention to detail and organizational skills. They are people-people.

Routine characteristics do not **only** apply to their jobs, but also to many aspects of their lives. The Craftsman is a creature of habit. A person with strong Craftsman traits may eat the same food, wear the same type of clothing, and repeat the same routine all day long without complaint. Stress emerges when any part of that routine changes.

Cursed by the ability to know every detail, the Craftsman must exercise tolerance to permit the rest of the world to understand them. People oriented, the Craftsman can easily show their emotions by talking a lot, laughing, crying, hugging and touching others in public. Showing concern for others, they enjoy being part of a team rather than working alone.

The Craftsman tends to trust others without reserve. This trait can be good or bad. They always want to think the best of people, and they try to help others whenever possible. This personality style makes great volunteers.

As a negative trait, the old adage: 'There is a sucker born every minute,' applies to them. Unfortunately, they seem to be the biggest target for every scam in existence. Extending trust to others makes them gullible. They often believe 'something must be true' if it is found on the Internet or in print. *The National Enquirer* magazine would not survive without the Craftsman.

Conservative in many ways, the Craftsman dresses, thinks and behaves in predictable ways. They attend church as an extension of their social needs. As a religious follower, they think of the scriptures as a giant 'rule book' teaching people the best way to live their lives.

A Craftsman is often viewed by others as a penny-pincher, tightwad, or just plain cheap due to their spending habits. However, they have a tough time resisting a sale on anything. The Craftsman believes if it's a 'good deal,' they must buy it, because it's too good to pass up, needed or not. This perspective usually results in a house full of stuff, so they have a garage sale every year to sell all the unneeded items they have accumulated. And these things are purchased by other Craftsman personalities who see the value in the purchase, turning this into a 'vicious cycle.'

A Craftsman will talk excessively. When conversing with a Craftsman by phone, the non-Craftsman listens more than speaks. In fact, the person on the other end of the line can put down the phone, take a bathroom break, make a sandwich, return to the phone, mutter "uh-huh," and the Craftsman will never know the other person was gone because they talked the entire time. But be careful, these folks are sensitive. Never criticize a Craftsman for these traits. They fear loss of security and personal rejection.

Because they are uncomfortable with change, they can be the employee who can turn his job into a career. Risk-taking frightens them. They prefer to play it safe and rely on job benefits to support family and personal goals. Having a good medical and dental plan, along with injury or death insurance and a good pension makes the Craftsman an excellent, content employee.

CUE WORDS TO DESCRIBE THE CRAFTSMAN

Patient	Good follower
Easygoing, relaxed	Steady
Excels with routine	Persistent
Cooperative, agreeable	Amiable
Family oriented	Occasionally uncertain
Detailed oriented	Upset by conflict/loves harmony

BEHAVIORAL TENDENCIES

- Can do repetitious tasks for hours
- Relaxed and in harmony with the world around them
- Will stick to a task with a persistence to accomplish it

FEARS

- Loss of security
- Fear of rejection

The Craftsman's personality traits can be seen in movie and television characters, often as the 'good buddies' of the main character, or they can become the foil for the clever antics of the star. TV characters who are typical Craftsmen tend to be sidekicks, like Edith Bunker on *All in the Family* or Al on *Home Improvement* or Norm and Cliff on *Cheers*. The current TV show, *The Big Bang Theory* has a host of Craftsman characters. It's like watching *Craftsmen Gone Wild!*

The Craftsman prefers to be 'the last one through the door' rather than the first one to try something new. They follow the path of the 'tried and true,' the 'Old Faithful' version of life. The Craftsman is very loyal and they perceive 'the norm' to be perfectly acceptable.

VALUABLE TIDBIT: They must feel you are mainly concerned with their feelings and security. Also, in the story of the tortoise and the hare they are the tortoise—so be very patient with them.

10

The Persuader Personality

Persuaders love the spotlight, literally and figuratively. Natural leaders, they are the first to take the initiative and want to be 'in charge' of everything. This personality style enjoys any type of challenge and approaches life by competing with everything and everyone.

They project a mental attitude of 'Never Give Up' on anything.

The 'never give up' attitude explains why they succeed in life so well. The thought of failing never enters their mind. When success is not immediate, the Persuader will try again and again until the goal is accomplished.

Great commission-based sales people have a combination of personality traits found in both the Driver and Persuader. They take advantage of every opportunity, have confidence in their ability to succeed, focus on the completion of goals, and pursue life with a positive mental attitude. They view everyday rejection as *a matter of timing* rather than a "No."

Persuaders work the crowd with kindness, good manners and a sterling sense of humor. Optimism rules their life. Others like to be in their company. Genuine in nature, they laugh, cry, smile, hug and touch others with ease. Dripping with charisma, the Persuader attracts loyal followers who gladly accept the Persuader's knack for leadership, decision-making and political savvy.

Status is *very important* to Persuaders. They show prominence in their possessions, clothes, houses or their many various 'toys' and purchases. They surround themselves with friends, business associates and even spouses or dating partners who enjoy an esteemed public reputation.

Designer logos were created for the Persuader. They love to display elegant brand names, the more visible the better! Wearing a chic brand lets everyone know they paid a lot for quality, and no further explanation is necessary.

The Persuader's personality can range from the 'high Persuader,' which includes the person who brags incessantly about themselves and their accomplishments, to the person who is the humble hero, unique but modest.

CUE WORDS TO DESCRIBE THE PERSUADER

Optimistic	Understanding
Enthusiastic	Encouraging
Persuasive	Outgoing
Popular	Sociable
Sees good in others	Friendly
Enjoys people	Shares feelings
Concern for people	Wants everyone to like them
Status is very important	People oriented
Excessive spending	Looks for opportunities
Natural leader	Charismatic

BEHAVIORAL TENDENCIES

- Wants and NEEDS to be liked
- Can relate to another person's point of view

- Likes to promote ideas
- 'Blue sky' approach to life
- Knows a great many people and tends to have a lot of acquaintances, rather than a few close friends.

FEARS

- Not being liked
- Being inadequate

Well known/famous Persuaders include: Madonna, Cher, Lady Gaga, Jimmy Fallon, Bill Clinton, John Wayne, Britney Spears, Elvis Presley, Oprah Winfrey, Ellen DeGeneres, Jay Leno, Sir Elton John, Sir Paul McCartney and most politicians. The list of public figures is quite long but their personality types are quite similar.

11

More Trait Recognition

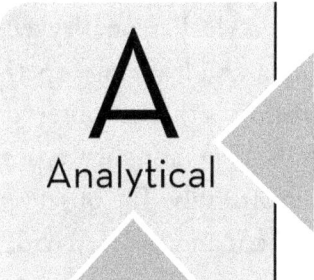
A Analytical

Colorless
Dull
Dark
Loners
Serious
Calm

D Driver

ASKS
Prefers the "Natural" Version, Detail Oriented, Employees, Slow-Paced

TELLS
Prefers the "Enhanced" Version, Bottom-Line Oriented, Employers, Fast-Paced

C Craftsman

Colorful
Friendly
Social
Fun-Loving
Emotional

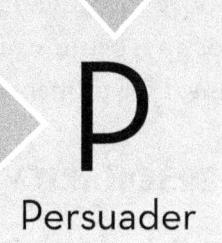
P Persuader

DESCRIPTIONS OF EACH PERSONALITY.

EXTRAPOLATION

A rough translation: to take a fact or characteristic, expand it and apply it to other characteristics.

Application makes personality recognition interesting, eye-opening, and relevant to many things throughout life. It can be applied to circumstances not only related to sales, but to every action and situation one encounters.

Every individual has their own unique personality style. Personality recognition becomes a lifelong type of entertainment and learning experience. The amazing aspect of personality recognition is that an observer will have the power to recognize each of the four personality types, immediately categorize them and act or react accordingly. The observer will be empowered to connect with a potential client and succeed without difficulty.

Recognition of a particular trait is important, but understanding *why* that trait is often related to a specific personality or two personalities is even more essential. In other words—*the psychology* and/or *motives* that cause that trait to occur are very important!

Something that makes personality recognition even more a part of your life—to help you relate particular traits/actions to a single type—use yourself as a great 'barometer.' Once you realize what mixture of personality types YOU are—and be very honest with yourself—you can enjoy realizing traits, that relate to a particular type and you'll know the motive. Because if you realize that something you like/don't like, do/not do is because of a certain type—guess what? = other people of that same type probably behave the same way!

PERSONALITY TRAIT REFERENCE GUIDE

D = Driver / P = Persuader / C = Craftsman / A = Analytical
VISUAL Clues: (actions, clothing, personal items, general appearance)

D/P:	More stylish and/or more 'classy.'
WHY:	They prefer the: best/unique/one-of-a-kind/newest, etc.
A/C:	Often satisfied with 'average' (at times—even below average).
WHY:	Choices are usually based on cost.
C/P:	More physical and outgoing—touching/hugging, etc.
WHY:	Anything that shows emotion.
A/C:	More likely to be overweight (a little or a lot).
WHY:	Being overweight is close to being *average* in American culture. Plus, they usually *lack the willpower* to say "no" to many delicious food items.
A/C :	More likely to wear glasses (vs. contacts or have corrective eye surgery).
WHY:	Primarily cost, but if glasses are seen as a fashion statement, P's will wear them to attract attention.
A/C:	More likely to wear caps (vs. stylish hats).
WHY:	Psychologically for protection, but also because their friends often wear caps, and it has become a comfortable habit. It is also very informal.
D/P:	More likely to be considered attractive by others.
WHY:	At some point, possibly as a young child, D/Ps realize they are naturally different from their *more average* peers: looks, intelligence, assertiveness, athletics etc.; an awareness that makes them behave differently. They assume leadership roles, express more confidence and more unique thoughts and actions. They like what they see in the mirror and can spend a great deal of money to keep a youthful, attractive look—even becoming candidates for plastic surgery in their latter years.

A/C: Prefer the *natural* attitude towards *everything* (nothing artificial).

WHY: A combination of: cost, being satisfied with *average* and contentment with *'the way it has always been done.'*

A/C: Males will sometimes have facial hair (beards). Usually, the longer the beard, the stronger the trait.

WHY: This choice corresponds with their *natural* attitude toward many things. If a Persuader has facial hair, it is very likely to be a trimmed goatee, because it is perceived as more unique or classy looking.

12

Levels of Personality Traits

There are many different 'levels' of each personality style, and even those intensities can shift from moment to moment, depending upon the circumstances.

A person is usually a mixture of two different types (sometimes even three, but never all four types). Various situations, stress levels, moods or settings may cause one or more levels of a personality style to emerge.

For instance, at one moment a person who is a Persuader/Craftsman can display more of their 'Persuader side' because they are making a sales call. But a few minutes later, they may be buying gasoline and choose a gas station which sells it a little cheaper than other stations. The 'Craftsman side' takes charge of their thinking at that moment. This shift in thinking and action occurs more often between the Driver/Analytical sides or the Persuader/Craftsman side of individuals.

A helpful hint: picture the image shown below.

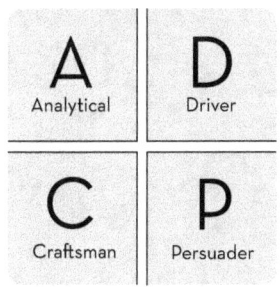

Confusion between the Driver and Persuader or the Analytical and Craftsman often occurs, mainly due to their titles. It may help to think of the different types in the following way. As in the image, there is only a thin line separating a 'low Driver' and a 'high Persuader' or a 'low Analytical and a high Craftsman.' That is very close to reality because those types (especially on the left or right side of the image) are actually extremely similar.

SIMILARITIES BETWEEN THE DRIVER AND PERSUADER BOTH ARE *EQUAL* IN:

- Leadership qualities
- Preferring a faster pace = "Get things done quickly"
- Not caring about the details
- Risk taking
- Being very goal oriented, competitive, and having a 'never give up' philosophy (*both are very 'driven' individuals*)

SIMILARITIES OF THE ANALYTICAL AND CRAFTSMAN. BOTH ARE *EQUAL* IN:

- Being *'analytically minded'* and extremely detail oriented
- Taking a long time to make decisions
- Being very cautious / careful
- Preferring to have a low risk associated with everything (guarantees are major)
- Being very routine oriented (and ideally—NO changes in their lives)

TWO BIG *DIFFERENCES* BETWEEN THE DRIVER AND ANALYTICAL VERSUS THE PERSUADER AND CRAFTSMAN ARE:

- The Persuader and Craftsman are 'people-people' and very social.
- The Persuader and Craftsman readily show emotions. (Laughing, crying, touching and hugging, etc.)

Neither of these traits apply to the Driver or Analytical!

13

Wants and Needs

People are motivated by opportunities to satisfy desires which are important and meaningful *to them*. People know what they consciously *want*, but not necessarily what they subconsciously *need*. When 'selling' a person a product or service, successful salespeople will concentrate more on the client's wants. If the sales person can satisfy the client's wants first, it becomes much easier to turn the want into a need, resulting in a probable sale.

A DRIVER WANTS:

- Power and authority
- Prestige and position
- Money and material things
- A challenge
- Opportunity for advancement results
- To know WHY or WHAT will be the 'end result' vs HOW. (They DO NOT care about the details regarding *'how'* they achieve that result)
- A wide scope of operation
- Direct answers

- Freedom from controls, supervision, and detail
- Efficiency of operation—they DO NOT like to wait for things
- New and varied activities

A DRIVER NEEDS:

- To know the results that are expected
- To have empathy (towards others)
- An occasional 'SHOCK' (being told a planned action is a BAD idea)

More than anyone else, a Driver can develop *'tunnel vision.'* Focused only on the end result, they proceed *'headlong'* towards that goal, not knowing or caring about what may happen to others as a result of their actions.

The Persuader will be the one who gives the Driver the 'shock' because the Analytical or Craftsman would not choose to stand up to a Driver, and suggest their actions are wrong. Another Driver would not intervene because two Drivers often think alike, so they both would see 'nothing wrong.'

Support their **actions** to establish rapport.

A PERSUADER WANTS:

- Popularity
- Social recognition
- Status
- Freedom from control and detail (they want someone else to 'do the chores')

A PERSUADER NEEDS:

- Control of time
- Personal financial management

Support their **intuition** (feelings) and their **'dreams'** to establish rapport. 'Painting a picture' of them using or owning the product or service can be beneficial.

A CRAFTSMAN WANTS:

- Status quo
- Security of the situation
- To collect things—(antiques, classic cars, stamps, etc.)
- A happy home life
- Historical procedures
- Sincerity
- A limited territory (the key word is limited = more DEFINED vs. WIDE)
- A long time to adjust to change
- Constant appreciation

A CRAFTSMAN NEEDS:

- Conditioning prior to change (think 'baby steps'— nothing 'sudden')
- Shortcut methods (They may NEED to be told of a quicker way to accomplish a task they have been doing for a long time.)

- Packaged presentation (Think of a '#4 menu choice' that has three items already chosen for the client.)
- Reassurance

Support their **feelings** to establish rapport.

AN ANALYTICAL WANTS:

- Standard operating procedures (step 1, step 2, etc. and they LOVE lists)
- Security (protection) = safety
- References
- Reassurance
- No sudden or abrupt changes
- To be told what to do
- Door openers. They *do not* want to be 'trailblazers' (the first people to buy/try something new)

AN ANALYTICAL NEEDS:

- Precision work
- Planning
- More confidence
- Wide angle and more perspective (vs. a narrow focus)
- Explanations and more explanation

Support presentations with **accurate data** and be very **precise**.

14

DOs and DON'Ts

The following information displays things the salesperson should ideally DO and NOT DO when selling to the various personality types. Unfortunately, some or many of the 'DON'Ts' occur during a sale, causing the presentation to end in failure without knowing why. **Success will come much easier if the salesperson emphasizes the Do's.**

TO SUCCESSFULLY PRESENT TO A DRIVER, DO THE FOLLOWING:

- Be clear, specific, brief, and to the point. **Don't** ramble on or waste their time.

- Stick to business. **Don't** insist on building a personal relationship.

- Present the facts logically and make your presentation efficiently. **Don't** leave loopholes or 'cloudy' issues.

- Ask specific (preferably '*what*') questions. **Don't** ask rhetorical questions (questions where you already know the answer).

- Provide alternatives and choices for making their own selections (options). **Don't** present a ready-made selection, nor make it for them.

- Provide facts and figures about probability of success or effectiveness of the options. **Don't** speculate wildly or offer guarantees and assurances.

- If you disagree, take issue with the facts, NOT THE PERSON. **Don't** let anything reflect on the client personally.

- If you agree, support the *results*, not the person. **Don't** reinforce thoughts with "I'm with you."

- After concluding the sale, part graciously. **Don't** launch into an epilogue after finishing business.

TO SUCCESSFULLY PRESENT TO A PERSUADER, DO THE FOLLOWING:

- Plan sales presentations that support their dreams and intuitions. **Don't** legislate, insist, or stand on 'policy.'

- Leave time for relating and socializing. **Don't** present in a curt, cold, or 'tight-lipped' manner.

- Talk about people, their goals and opinions they find stimulating. **Don't** waste time trying to be impersonal, judgmental, or task-oriented.

- Ask for *their* opinions and ideas regarding people. **Don't** talk down to the client.

- Use enough time to be stimulating, fun, fast moving, and entertaining. **Don't** kid around, nor stick to the agenda too much.

- Provide testimonials from people they believe are important and/or prominent. **Don't** give the client the idea 'everyone is doing it,' or use a testimonial from someone that they would consider as being an *average* person.

TO SUCCESSFULLY PRESENT TO A CRAFTSMAN, DO THE FOLLOWING:

- Start, however briefly, with a personal comment to 'break the ice.' **Don't** rush headlong into a sales presentation.

- Show sincere interest in them as people; find areas of common involvement. Be candid and open. **Don't** stick coldly or harshly to business or lose sight of goals by being too personal.

- Patiently draw out preferences and work with them to help satisfy these tastes. Listen and be responsive. **Don't** force them to respond quickly to your presentation. **Don't** say: "Here is how **I** see it."

- Present your case softly and non-threateningly. **Don't** become domineering or demanding.

- Ask "*how?*" questions to draw out their opinions. **Don't** debate facts and figures.

- If you disagree, look for hurt feelings and personal reasons. Be compassionate. **Don't** patronize or demean by using subtlety or cunning.

- Move casually and informally. **Don't** be abrupt and rapid.

- Provide guarantees that their selection is optimal and carries very little risk. **Don't** offer assurances and guarantees that can't be fulfilled.

- Offer special, immediate and extra incentives for willingness to buy now! Focus and then close in a timely manner. **Don't** leave the sales presentation open-ended.

TO SUCCESSFULLY PRESENT TO AN ANALYTICAL, DO THE FOLLOWING:

- Approach them in a straightforward direct way, and stick to business. **Don't** present a circuitous, roundabout, giddy, casual, informal, or loud behavior.

- Support their principles. Build your credibility by listing pros and cons to any suggestion you make. **Don't** rush the decision-making process with pressure to buy. Help make the choice obvious.

- Make an organized contribution to their efforts and present specifics. **Don't** be vague about what the product can do and follow through on commitments.

- Take your time, but be persistent and focus. **Don't** dilly-dally.

- Make an organized presentation of your product's strength. **Don't** make a personal appeal to obtain a sale.

- Provide solid, tangible, practical evidence. **Don't** use someone's opinion (vs. facts) as evidence.

- Indicate guarantees over a long period, but provide options (but you MUST close on them at the original presentation). **Don't** use gimmicks or clever, quick manipulations.

15

Personality Percentages

Before examining the research data on personality types, guess the percentage of individuals in the United States who have each personality style.

DRIVER: _____ %

PERSUADER: _____ %

ANALYTICAL: _____ %

CRAFTSMAN: _____ %

Make sure the total equals 100%.

Now look at the Research findings on personality types in the chart on the next page: Any surprises?

- Driver .... 9% of the population
- Persuader. ... 11% of the population
- Analytical .... 30% of the population
- Craftsman ... 50% of the population

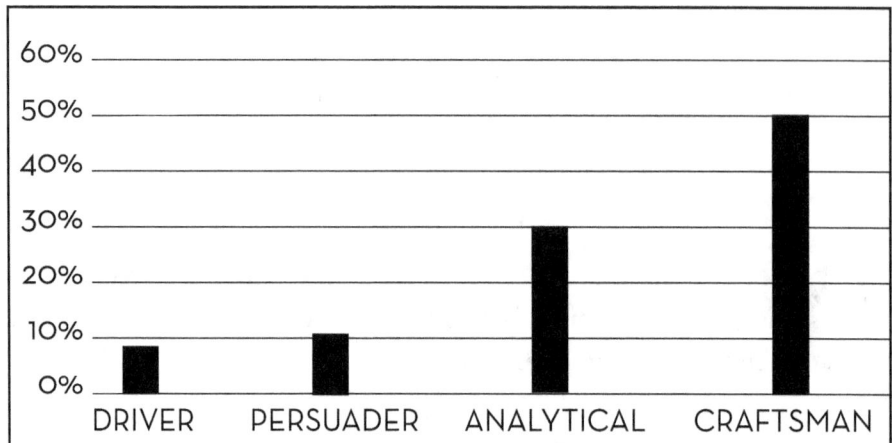

Amazingly, this research supports the Pareto Principle—better known as 'The 80/20 rule.' Twenty percent represent the LEADERS (**D/P**), and eighty percent represent the FOLLOWERS (**A/C**). Similar to a large corporation or factory setting, the management staff is small compared to the number of 'average' employees in the factory. Only a few **D/Ps** are needed to lead or manage a large amount of **A/Cs**.

(I totally agree with the 80/20 rule, but I feel there are even more of the Persuader and Craftsman because I think most people are 'people-people,' friendly, caring, etc. I feel the percentages should be closer to five percent Driver and fifteen percent Persuader, and twenty percent Analytical and sixty percent Craftsman.)

In commission sales, the Persuader and Driver usually lead the way, but can be extremely effective selling and presenting to the Craftsman and Analytical **if** they apply personality insights, approaches and strategies that work most effectively with the other personality types. Knowledge makes one an effective and very successful salesperson.

PART THREE

Extra Valuable Tidbits

16

Match the Personality to the Job

Many businesses experience a high turnover rate with sales representatives. After much time, money, and training, management becomes frustrated and disappointed because the company's mentoring efforts failed to have a long-term impact on success.

Such examples of failure can frequently be traced to hiring the wrong people (personality types) to accomplish intended goals. Without using the knowledge and insights of personality patterns, many companies hire the Craftsman to do jobs designed to guarantee success for the Persuader.

When focused on sales or the presentation of ideas, one strong Persuader can provide as much business as ten employees with Craftsman traits in a *commission based* sales job. Hiring the wrong personality style is like betting on a snail to win a race that is based solely upon speed. It doesn't work.

An Analytical or Craftsman will soar in a job that requires patience, precision and repetition. If they will also be required to deal with the public, a Craftsman should meet and greet the public. The Craftsman is a 'people-person,' while an Analytical is driven solely by data and should be kept out of sight.

Place an Analytical in a windowless room, assign them a job to file boxes with papers, and they will love it because they understand the task and can see when the goal is achieved. Besides, with nobody to bother them, the Analytical can probably accomplish the job in a shorter amount of time, be refreshed and ready to handle the next task.

The Craftsman or Analytical will never become a star (commission) salesperson in the company. Both types prefer a guaranteed *salary* which provides them with clearly identified employee benefits such as insurance, profit sharing, and/or a retirement plan. A job with no risks becomes much more appealing.

On the other hand, Drivers and Persuaders can handle, even prefer, *commission* jobs, unless they are paid a high salary, reserved mostly for elite executives. Company bonuses, often based upon sales results, make the job even more appealing.

Drivers and Persuaders do not need, even disdain, to be micro-managed. They desire to be 'turned loose' to do their own thing. They love to achieve goals assigned by management and really thrive when given permission to set their own goals. Persuaders are 'people-people,' and can become great mentors for other salespeople, if they don't mind sharing their expertise.

Unlike Persuaders, Drivers are not 'people-people' and prefer to work alone, especially when placed in a selling situation. They are not team players and chafe at the thought of collaboration with others. They want to run their part of the business their way with little or no interference from others.

Both Drivers and Persuaders can easily assume a leadership role. When placed in that position, Drivers are more 'feared' by people below them in rank, while Persuaders are more respected and well-liked. Both types are very 'control-oriented' people.

A common phrase you will often hear from a Driver in a leadership role is *"It's my way or the highway!"* The Persuader's given name is very appropriate because they are usually skilled in the 'art of persuasion.'

VALUABLE TIDBIT: Clearly know who to hire and clarify expectations for them based on their personality style.

17

Advertising to the Different Personality Types

Various sources indicate that the total for all advertising expenses in the U.S. in 2017 was over $206,000,000,000. That's $206 billion with a capital B. In addition, a 30 second ad during the 2018 Super Bowl cost more than $5 million. That equals more than $165,000 per second.

According to the Gartner Business Research Study, the average company spends slightly more than 10% of their budget on advertising. The best way a company can obtain the highest return on their investment (ROI), which they always strive for, is to first ask, *'What is my client's prime personality type?'*

And based upon the insight of the prospective client, you can then answer other important questions:

- What <u>motivates</u> them to buy or act?
- What is the <u>best form of advertising</u> to reach them? (via audio, video, a written message, television, radio or online)
- What exact advertiser represents the <u>best ad placement</u> for them? For example: if advertising on TV—which station, time of day, during which shows, etc.

- What <u>subject matter</u> should be addressed in the advertising?
- What are the <u>best words</u> to use to 'grab their attention'?

It's quite a bit to consider, but the time spent examining the approach that works best for the client will be worthwhile in the long run.

The best way to demonstrate this point is to examine a common advertising practice that occurs every month, and it is helpfully delivered by the United Postal Service: The Coupon Book.

The target market for ANY money-saving coupon book is the Craftsman or Analytical because they love 'deals.' One of their main buying motives is to save money. Coupons are *their thing*. They diligently read through every page of a coupon book to see if they can snag a bargain—any bargain.

However, when the Driver or Persuader receives a coupon book in the mail, their first reaction is to deposit it, unread, in the trash because saving money is of no concern to them. They believe coupon books are for 'those other people' who need such bargains. Using or even receiving a coupon book is an insult because they express an 'I don't need it' attitude.

For example, if a Driver or a Persuader received a coupon book offering a huge discount for six tanning sessions, they might show initial interest, but saving money is not a motivation for them. They look for instant results, no matter what price they have to pay.

Impressing others by looking good is of utmost importance. Instead of buying a tanning membership, they may even fly to Mexico for the weekend, returning with a tan that would impress others.

A great deal of time and money is spent designing, developing, printing and distributing discount coupons. But coupons can represent wasted marketing dollars if they get into the hands of the wrong clients.

One day, I visited a tanning salon which advertised in a local coupon book. I asked the teenage girl behind the counter if they had customers use the coupons on a regular basis.

"Oh yes, we use them quite often," she said.

I thought this was odd and asked, "Do you mean you have a lot of people bring in the coupons?"

She replied, "Well, if the client doesn't mention the coupon immediately, I have a box of them under the counter, and I give them one to use during their visit." (Appropriate response = open hand slaps forehead!)

Now think about this: Because the client is primarily a Persuader or Driver, they *don't care* about saving money! They just want to get a quick tan and look good.

The client had already made the decision to come to that business. The client had walked in the door, not to 'look around' but to get a tan.

Obviously, the young employee behind the counter was a Craftsman who cared a lot about *saving money* and *helping others*, so she was satisfying both of her 'inner motives' at the same time.

The owner probably went through the cash register at the end of the day, saw the stack of used coupons and said to themselves, "This is a fantastic way to advertise. I'm going to keep doing this." But the business might as well have thrown that part of the advertising budget into the trash!

On the flip side, I once saw two ads that were placed alongside each other in a newspaper. One ad contained a list of the current best-selling books, and the other ad was touting a CD investment at a local bank with a 3.25% return.

The placement was excellent! Was it just 'luck' or smart ad placement? Both the Craftsman and the Analytical represent the major market for book sales AND may be interested in a safe, guaranteed 3.25 % return CD.

VALUABLE TIDBIT: Invest advertising dollars more wisely by targeting messages to the wants and needs of your best client's personality types.

18

Choosing a Seat at the Table

It doesn't matter if you are selling yourself, a product, an idea or a service—the salesperson should make the most of every item that can be controlled. This strategy *includes* the seating arrangement, the shape of the table and where people sit. The successful placement of people can influence the outcome of the presentation.

The shape of the table or desk and the location of chairs at those tables strongly correlate with the tasks to be performed and the psychology of the situation. Whether the purpose of the conference is an interview, a formal meeting, an informal chat, a hopeful sale or a negotiation, the selection of seating and the placement of the people involved requires major consideration.

Several examples demonstrate this concept:

A boss will often have a huge desk where an interview is conducted. The interviewee often will be seated across from the boss—possibly even in a smaller chair. Sitting behind a large desk or at the head of a conference table denotes power, prestige and status. The Driver, as boss, seeks to impress and believes bigger and more expensive is better. Persuaders follow the same path when they want to flaunt wealth or power.

The Driver and Persuader seek recognition as the definitive leader and authority figure in the room. They want to leave *no doubt* they are the person *in charge*. The Driver boss may even have their office chair raised up or constructed higher than the other chairs in the room in order to be looking down on others, a leftover vestige of royalty.

To promote equality and encourage honest dialogue, a round table puts people at ease and psychologically enhances balance in the meeting. At a round table, every voice shares equal status and balance.

One of the most famous examples of the circular table seating arrangement was The Knights of the Round Table. King Arthur, without any doubt, was a Persuader rather than a Driver because he joined his knights in discussions at the round table. While seated at that table, no person ranked higher than anyone else. Every person was considered equal, and each knight could voice their opinion without the worry of being 'out-of-line.' King Arthur risked a great deal to make himself seem equal to his loyal knights, but psychologically, he preserved power by sharing it.

Another Persuader, Jacqueline Kennedy, introduced round banquet tables to the White House state dinners. The smaller round tables encouraged more conversation than the traditional large U-shaped tables that once dominated the banquet hall.

VALUABLE TIDBIT: In a meeting, choose a seat wisely. Identify who is in charge and everyone's role. By clarifying the purpose of the meeting, the correct seating will provide the physical and psychological edge to achieve intended outcomes.

If your intention is to sell a product or service to your client, *avoid a 'confrontational' seating arrangement* (where you and the client are on opposite sides of the table). Even when sitting at the corner of a rectangular table, consider the corner as a 'wall.' Try to avoid as much separation as possible. Salespeople want to be perceived as a friend not a 'coercive enemy.' Remember, *it's all psychological*.

19

Bosses

Drivers and Persuaders make up the dominant leadership types because they are both concerned with the end results. However, each style attains the completion of goals in different ways.

The Driver's focus on the bottom line motivates them to 'cut to the chase' and identify what it will cost to complete projects, make the most money and do it all in a short amount of time. They run roughshod over anything or anyone who gets in the way. **It is important to remember that individuals exhibit *different levels* of a personality trait.** The 'high' Driver leads through intimidation and/or force and is more feared.

Persuaders are 'people-people' and work toward completing goals in a friendly, collaborative manner. They tend to be more reachable by the average employee. Persuader bosses show concern for their employees in different ways, like using first names and creating a work environment that provides various employee benefits, incentive plans and family-friendly programs. The 'high' Persuader leads through positive personal interactions and is more respected.

The difference in types is one reason the Driver boss will often incur higher employee turnover over the long term compared to the Persuader boss. The Craftsman and Analytical types make up the vast majority of workers and will tolerate poor working conditions and office politics for a long time because they try to avoid change. However, once the job becomes intolerable and dissatisfaction with working conditions becomes epidemic, the exit stampede begins in earnest in the Driver-run business and 'the domino effect' takes over.

VALUABLE TIDBIT: Check out the work environment and culture before trying to sell or present anything to a Driver or Persuader boss. Be sure you know what personality style you are dealing with.

20

Two Ears and One Mouth

The best commission salespeople are excellent listeners and the best listeners are Persuaders. They listen much more than the Drivers. Although both personality types do quite well at commission sales, they often use their listening talents for different things.

The Persuader cares about others and usually listens to their clients. They focus on the client's likes, dislikes, family, habits, activities and recreational choices. Persuaders listen for ways to connect to the client beyond the business of selling.

The Driver's main concern is all about making their **OWN** point! Drivers only think about the profit in the sale and control the conversation. Their goal is to win, to close, and to move on to the next client.

The salesperson's 'time' in a selling situation can often **unfortunately** be compared to a pyramid. From the top, down, it represents a shorter introduction, resulting in a time-consuming close.

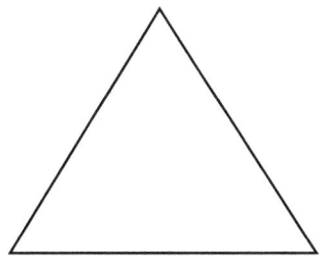

To be an effective commission salesperson, his/her personality style must be at least half Driver or Persuader in order to have that 'never give up' attitude which, by definition, is a necessary requirement of sales.

Because Drivers and Persuaders generally lack patience, they often rush into the sales process and expect a quick close. Unfortunately the opposite is often the case.

What the salesperson *perceives to be 'the close'* of the sale results in the client essentially saying, "Yes, *but*" over and over again and the 'quick sale' turns into a marathon event!

Timing and effective communication may get lost in the process. The salesperson often asks the client, "Why didn't you mention these things earlier?" And the client's response is likely to be, "You never asked."

A more efficient and much less stressful approach for both parties can be represented by an **inverted** pyramid (or funnel) shape. From the top down, this strategy utilizes a longer introduction, hopefully ending in a quicker close.

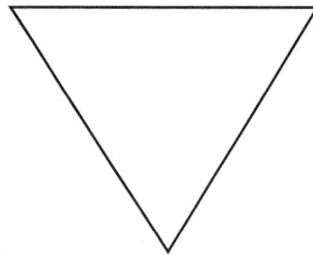

This approach utilizes several *open-ended questions* at the beginning of the conversation—questions like: "What are your goals?", or "What do you want to achieve with/from this?", or "What is more important in making your decision—budget or obtaining the best/most exclusive product or service available?"—permit the salesperson to focus on how to make the most effective presentation.

By recognizing the personality style of the client, wasting time can be avoided. The way the salesperson poses questions, and the vocabulary that's used will facilitate a much better presentation. By listening carefully to the client's needs and wants, the salesperson can use the best approach to achieving a sales goal.

We were all given two ears and only one mouth for a reason. Use them in that proportion! *Let the client tell you what they want and therefore 'how to sell them.'*

By listening carefully and responding correctly, the salesperson is less likely to hear "Yes, but" by showing the client how a particular choice perfectly fulfills the goals and desires *the client just expressed* in answers to the salesperson's *open-ended* questions.

The inverted 'pyramid approach' (or funnel approach) CAN lead to a much quicker and less stressful sale overall for BOTH parties!

VALUABLE TIDBIT: Listen carefully to the client and the words they use. Take careful note of the client's goals, wants and needs. Choose vocabulary that responds and satisfies those desires.

21

Sell—Don't Tell

This event took place in a small town's general store. Much like a big city department store, they carried a huge variety of merchandise. The store had been a fixture for at least thirty years, and only the owner managed the business. One summer, he decided to hire some extra help to enjoy some time off from his demanding six-day work week.

He hired a high school boy and trained him enough so the boy could become familiar with the merchandise and feel comfortable working on his own. One day, after the boy had been there for a few weeks, the old man asked the boy if he would mind if he left the store while he went home for lunch. The boy said, "Sure, take your time. I can handle everything. No problem."

The owner left to have lunch and to run a few errands. When the owner returned, he walked over to the cash register to see how the boy had done in his absence. To the man's surprise, the owner discovered the boy had sold more than $1,300 in product during his two hour absence.

The old man looked at the total on the cash register and assumed it was wrong. He thought the kid had made a *huge* mistake. The store had never sold that much merchandise so quickly.

He wanted the boy to explain. "You said you could handle everything if I left you alone for a while. The register shows you did far over $1,000 worth of business while I was gone. There is *no way* you could have done that much business in such a short time."

The boy replied, "I'm sure I rang up everything correctly. Besides, this one guy bought a *lot* of stuff!"

"Oh really," the owner said in disbelief. "Just what did he buy?"

"Well, let me think. He bought a tent, a lantern, a sleeping bag, a camp stove, a great rod and reel, a tackle box, a bunch of nice lures, a small raft with oars and a nice fishing hat with a matching fishing vest."

"All that!" The owner exclaimed in amazement. "Wow! A guy comes in to buy a tent, and *you sold him so much more*. Nice job!"

The kid hesitated for a few seconds and said, "Well, he originally came in the store looking for a pillow."

"A what?" the owner shouted. "But, you said he bought all that merchandise."

'True," the boy replied, "but when he first came in, he asked if we had any pillows for sale."

"Pillows?"

"I told him that we had several types of pillows, and we started talking about different types."

The owner listened carefully, not knowing where the boy was headed.

"Then he mentioned his mother-in-law planned to visit for a few days, so he needed an extra pillow." The boy smiled and added, so I said, "Do you know what would be a great idea and lots of fun? You should take a few days and go fishing!"

The boy smiled at the owner and both grinned. The owner shook the boy's hand and said, "Great salesmanship!"

This story emphasizes the difference between SELLING and TELLING.

If the kid had been a Craftsman, like the owner, the client would have left the store with **only** a brand new pillow. However, the kid, obviously a Persuader, listened carefully to the man's NEEDS and showed him how to make the most of the mother-in-law's visit.

VALUABLE TIDBIT: Listen to the client to hear their needs and wants, and then sell them products or services based on what you hear.

22

The Art of Mirroring

Practicing a speech or exercising can be enhanced by watching yourself in front of a mirror. But the term *'mirroring'* in a sales situation is about copying the client, both physically and verbally.

The basic premise of *personality recognition* is that people will relate, be more receptive to ideas or opinions, even buy, if they believe the salesperson is *like them*. The client's perception may be totally subconscious, but the result is often *precisely* what the salesperson intended.

One method of *mirroring* is through body language. There is no need to copy the client's body language *exactly*. However, a similar form of body language is recommended. Mirroring body language exactly will probably make the client feel uncomfortable, or even get upset, but if it can be accomplished through subtle changes and go unnoticed, the action will achieve positive results.

If the client's body language sends negative signals such as crossed arms or legs, it may help if the salesperson behaves in a similar fashion for a short time to establish a rapport. Then, the salesperson should gradually change to a more positive and open position. If it doesn't succeed the first time, revert to the prior body language, wait a few moments, and try again.

After mirroring the client for a while, the salesperson should change their own body language. If the client feels connected to the salesperson, the client will often begin mirroring the salesperson's movements.

For example, if the salesperson moves forward, or uncrosses legs or arms, and the client begins to mirror that behavior, this indicates the client is more receptive and 'on the same wave length' so to speak. This should be a signal to the salesperson to *move toward closure.*

The strategy of mirroring is not limited to only body language. Mirroring can also apply to the clothing, physical appearance and even verbal or written expressions. Mirroring assists the salesperson's initial goal to establish a rapport with the client. The best way to achieve this is to appear 'just like them' in various ways.

People feel most comfortable and therefore more apt to 'make a purchase' with people they view as similar to themselves. Examples of more mirroring include:

Verbal expressions: If the salesperson agrees with the other person's point of view, use **similar** adjectives such as *fantastic, wonderful, great* or vice versa—*poor, lousy, ridiculous,* etc.

Written expressions: Use a similar font, sentence structure, page layout, punctuation, salutation and ending comment when emailing. This often works quite well, without them even recognizing it. When the client reads the salesperson's replies in the same format, font and word structure, they will tend to relate to the salesperson even more.

Physical appearance: Especially if *the average client is* physically fit, the salesperson should be as well. When representing a product or service which promises a more positive physical appearance, the salesperson should model the expected result themselves.

Haircuts: Mirror the client with either a stylish or an average look.

Clothing: If applicable, match the client with a professional look (a suit and tie). If the dress is informal, match conservative with conservative and vice versa. Some exceptions may occur in a leader who does not care what others think, or when they want to stand out from the crowd and be recognized for that quality. Be aware of dress and act accordingly.

VALUABLE TIDBIT: Mirror, Mirror on the wall: Earn their trust by mirroring it all!

23

Have A Good One!

Those four words make up one of the most common phrases expressed by a Craftsman when you leave their presence. The phrase is spoken many times every day by checkout clerks and bank tellers—all Craftsmen. The redundancy makes it become a meaningless phrase to the client, ignored and forgotten by both people.

The Craftsman says this phrase so often and so automatically, they don't even think about it or realize it. It is a habit and *they* can be *major* 'creatures of habit.'

A few years ago, I decided to conduct a quick 'experiment' to verify my thoughts regarding Craftsmen saying this statement to people (over and over) as the other person is leaving.

I was making a deposit (inside) at my local bank. When I had finished the transaction and was leaving the teller, she uttered that standard Craftsman phrase, "have a good one". I had only taken 4 or 5 steps. I turned around and returned to the teller. I asked her "Can you tell me the last statement you JUST said to me as I was leaving"?

She made 2 or 3 guesses, but all were incorrect. I wasn't surprised at all! Because a Craftsman will usually say the phrase so automatically, they don't even think about what they are saying!

An analysis of why a person chooses those words, whether consciously or not, offers the salesperson an insight into the mind of the speaker.

Have: A 'passive' word, which is much like the Craftsman. By using the word 'have,' the speaker 'trusts the outcome to fate,' etc.

Good: This word denotes something is just 'average' in nature, much like the Craftsman's general level of satisfaction with everything. They feel that 'average,' in everything is good enough.

One: Consider the basic premise for a moment. The Craftsman feels very comfortable with *repetition*. They like, even prefer, things or circumstances that remain constant in nature. The Craftsman can utter this phrase ***all day*** and never have to change. The phrase simplifies life for them.

Using the phrase, *"Make it a great day"* changes one's perspective on life. Persuaders often use this statement because they have a different view of the world.

Make vs. Have: Encourages people to TAKE CONTROL of their destiny.

Great vs. Good: This represents a much better outcome, a higher level of accomplishment.

Day (or evening) **vs. One:** It is more specific.

Another frequently spoken Craftsman phrase that expresses little meaning are the words asked by a restaurant's waiter or waitress as they complete their rounds:

"Are you still working on that?"

The phrase is intended to ask if the patron is finished with the meal, but the hollow words detract and minimize the dining experience.

A Persuader, interested in the well-being of the client should be asking, "Are you still savoring your meal or have you finished?"

VALUABLE TIDBIT: Be more aware of the power of your words and the meaning you want to convey.

PART FOUR

Saving the Best for Last

24

Planning Your Sales Attack

If you have a meeting scheduled with someone, and you already know their personality style, it can help you quite a bit to look at the corresponding info here to improve your sales call or presentation.

(**Note:** I want to stress, DON'T feel you need to 'memorize' this information. Just get a 'good feel' for it and proceed accordingly.)

If a prospect's buying style is: a DRIVER, you can enhance their receptivity by:

STEPS	STRATEGY
PREPARATION	Emphasize immediate short-term benefits.
	Plan to appeal to prospect's need to achieve, win, and obtain competitive advantage.
GETTING ATTENTION	Be brief. Don't try to cover all benefits. Isolate the most 'dollar related' product advantage that can be verified, or the product benefit which provides the most competitive edge, and lead with

	that. (Say—"you will have the competitive edge if " . . .)
STYLE AWARENESS	Move fast. Recognize that the prospect is impatient. They may demonstrate a short attention span.
PRESENTATION	Use brief visuals—the more 'bottom-line' oriented, the better. Ask questions that involve the prospect. Make them talk and allow them to lead. (They want short-term benefits!)
STYLE OF RELATING	You must be enthusiastic, brief, and open-ended. Control, but don't force.
HANDLING OBJECTIONS	Answer objections quickly. Don't hesitate to 'fence' with the prospect because they like to 'test' you, guard against over-reacting.
CLOSE	Try to be brief and dramatic. You must ask for the order! Where possible, use an action close, emphasizing an immediate opportunity and give a sense of urgency.

■ ■ ■ ■

If a prospect's buying style is: a PERSUADER, you can enhance their receptivity by:

STEPS	STRATEGY
PREPARATION	Plan to approach on an informal, first-name basis, concentrating on developing a personal relationship with the prospect. Develop personal testimonial

references whenever possible from third parties that the prospect knows. Learn personal information from prospect.

GETTING ATTENTION — Be positive, enthusiastic and unstructured. Avoid any approach that may sound 'canned'.

STYLE AWARENESS — Emphasize interaction; try to develop a climate that approaches interesting and informal conversation.

PRESENTATION — Avoid a formal use of visuals. Testimonial information and slides are OK as long as they are 'woven-in' and are not used as 'a dog and pony show'.

STYLE OF RELATING — Be open. Don't try to gloss over weak points. Show respect and interest in the prospect as a person, first. You must have their authentic trust before they will buy.

HANDLING OBJECTIONS — Be sure to convey empathy and show that you can and do accept this prospect's feelings. Then respond factually to issues that they raise.

CLOSE — Avoid making a formal summary. Concentrate on the immediate next steps and assume that the prospect is favorably disposed and help them to buy—rather than asking them for the order 'straight out'. Try to 'back-door' the close. In other words—don't make it obvious.

If a prospect's buying style is: a CRAFTSMAN, you can enhance their receptivity by:

STEPS	STRATEGY
PREPARATION	Research the prospect's plans, especially growth and goal plans. Identify most innovative or special aspects of your product, and plan to show how these will benefit them, their family and their future.
GETTING ATTENTION	Ask several open questions, which force the prospect to reveal their plans. Then relate your product benefits to their game-plan.
STYLE AWARENESS	The prospect may go off on tangents —bring them back. Emphasize ways that will maximize customer's willingness to open up and talk at length.
PRESENTATION	Be selective, rather than structured. Ask them what aspects they would most like you to develop; then do so, using them as a 'sounding board', frequently seeking feedback.
STYLE OF RELATING	Be careful not to push or crowd. Convey respect for the prospect. They don't respond to 'sugar-coating', but they do appreciate being recognized.
HANDLING OBJECTIONS	Avoid arguing with the prospect. Remember that they like cooperation and stability. Probe all of their concerns.

CLOSE	Use a low-key, assumptive type of close where possible. This prospect does not like to be 'sold', but they do not object to having you help them execute their own strategy.

■ ■ ■ ■

If a prospect's buying style is: an ANALYTICAL, you can enhance their receptivity by:

STEPS	STRATEGY
PREPARATION	Emphasize research. Know the prospect's situation thoroughly. Be prepared and ready to cite facts. Have several alternative strategies in mind.
GETTING ATTENTION	Express yourself as logically and in a detailed systematic low-key fashion (as much as possible).
STYLE AWARENESS	Use a structured approach. The prospect probably tends to be detailed oriented, so emphasize 'thoroughness and completeness'. Solicit feedback.
PRESENTATION	Use visuals, charts, statistics, and leave-behind written documents. This prospect will read everything, usually thoroughly.
STYLE OF RELATING	You should be controlled, professional, and organized. This prospect is skeptical, especially of flamboyant styles or exaggerated claims.

HANDLING OBJECTIONS

Make sure you understand and probe objections. Take your time. Don't hesitate to defer responding to some of them immediately, as long as you indicate that you intend covering these in some detail at a later point.

CLOSE

Try to be thorough. Summarize and use your summaries whenever possible as a close. If the customer does not buy, try closing the other alternatives you have prepared.

■ ■ ■ ■

25

Dominant Buying Motives

What if you could 'read the minds' of your clients, or anyone for that matter, and know exactly WHY they would *buy* or *do* anything? *Imagine the power that would give a salesperson!*

The information contained on the following pages shares the keys to dominant buying motives. The client may not realize it immediately, or even want to admit it, but these are their dominant motives. For a salesperson this information is *solid gold*.

TREAT THIS LIKE GOLD!

Copy the chart on page 97 to keep with you for quick reference. Display it in 'strategic places' where it can be read EVERY DAY.

On your master bath mirror • In your wallet • In your car
Near the office phone, etc. • On your office desk.

This Dominant Buying Motives summary is perfect for preparation before a sales call or meeting of any kind, where the desired outcome is a successful 'close.'

One does *not* need to memorize all of these motives. A general understanding of the dominant motives of each style is sufficient. The main requirements to achieve tremendous success are these:

- Recognize the client's major personality style at that moment.

- Extrapolate the dominant buying motives that apply to the current situation.

- Make your sale!

VALUABLE TIDBIT: Looking at the dominant buying motives in detail, notice that the word 'avoid' is used six times when describing the Analytical and Craftsman, but zero times with the Driver and Persuader. That should tell you a lot. A's and C's 'avoid' things in life vs. the D or P, who are always striving to 'move ahead.' They love a 'challenge.'

DOMINANT BUYING MOTIVES

ANALYTICAL
- To fulfill physical needs
- To avoid trouble
- To be clean
- To save money
- To be accurate
- To avoid criticism
- To keep possessions
- To avoid physical pain
- To avoid loss of money
- To achieve comfort

DRIVER
- To take advantage of opportunity
- To be an individual
- The desire to gain
- To make money
- To have status
- To be emulated
- To have a challenge
- To own

CRAFTSMAN
- To emulate others
- To avoid loss
- To save money
- To be safe
- To promote family unity
- To avoid effort
- To have security
- To be comfortable

PERSUADER
- To have beautiful possessions
- To attract the opposite sex
- To gratify curiosity
- To enjoy pleasure
- To hold onto youth
- To be popular
- To be in style
- To be praised
- To have recognition

A Special Gift

The author, Ron Stickler, prides himself on making continued education a part of ongoing training in addition to the extensive personality recognition training acquired in this book.

As a special 'Thank You' for purchasing this book, and more importantly investing in the longevity of your business and career, we would like to invite you to join our private Facebook group.

Even if you are not a Facebook member, it would be well worth it to join Facebook, if only to gain access to this exclusive site that will help further your sales career.

Every week, Ron posts new and exciting tips, advice and coaching in the form of posts that all members can read and learn from. This is an ongoing gift to you—totally complimentary—with 'no strings attached.'

Go to https://www.facebook.com/groups/PROSPERITYpr/ and click on **JOIN** to start your ongoing enjoyment with weekly reminders of personality recognition.

When Ron receives your request, he will place you in the private group, and you can return to the site to view the 200 + posts that are already there and each new weekly post will be available to you.

You are encouraged to take 1 or 2 minutes each week to visit the site. This will help keep personality recognition continually on your mind as you experience everything around you—both personally and business-wise.

IMPORTANT NOTE: DO NOT write a 'comment' on any 'old post' because it will cause Facebook to reshuffle the order of the entire weekly posts (causing problems) and your membership in the group will be terminated by the administrator of the group.

Do you have a testimonial you would like to share? Send an email directly to ron@prosperitypersonalityrecognition.com and use TESTIMONIAL in the subject line.

Dedication

This book is dedicated to Ken Droney—my junior high school Algebra teacher. His 'thinking outside the box' methods of teaching immediately inspired me to consider teaching as a future goal. It took about 35 years to 'go full circle,' but I found myself teaching as a vocation, and hopefully making a difference in people's lives—as he did for me.

Acknowledgments

My wife (Patti), who listened to me continually talk about 'personalities' for the last 30 years.

Bill Lamperes, who without his continued assistance in editing and authoring advice, this book would have remained just a dream.

My past students and clients (especially Sean McCarthy) who have encouraged me for years to write a book about personality recognition.

Lisa Neuberger for the initial editing.

Robin Shukle and Liz Mrofka (of What If? Publishing) for the final editing and book design.

Now, Go Forth and REACH & EXCEED YOUR SALES GOALS FOREVER!

The information in this book CAN change your sales career—forever. It is unlike any other 'sales improvement' material you will probably ever receive because it is very unique, extremely simple and it is easy to quickly apply. You will immediately start to see the entire world around you differently. What is amazing is that, these things were always there—but now you see everything 'through different colored glasses' and you will have a totally different perspective.

You will know the 'motivating buying interests' of every client. That alone is the main reason I have NEVER received a referral *within* a company because when a commissioned salesperson learns this information, **they quickly realize they have a huge competitive edge,** and they DO NOT want to lose that edge.

As they say, 'knowledge is power' and this information can provide an *immense* feeling of power to the recipient.

www.ingramcontent.com/pod-product-compliance
Lightning Source LLC
Chambersburg PA
CBHW052331220526
45472CB00001B/375